String of Pearls ...
A Mother's Wisdom

by

Marie True Evans

GM BOOKS.COM

String of Pearls ... A Mother's Wisdom
by Marie True Evans

ISBN# 1882383-56-7

Graphics Management Press
10520 Ohio Avenue
Los Angeles, CA 90024
email: gm@graphics-management.com
(310) 475-2988 Fax (310) 475-9486

Project Director Anita Dorich
Book Design and Photography William Dorich
Text Editing Cliff Carle

Celebrity Photos:
Pearl Bailey—©Bettmann, Corbis
Barbara Bush—©Wally McNamee, Corbis
Lolita Davidovich—©Frank Trapper, Corbis/Sygma
Phyllis Diller—©Douglas Kirkland, Corbis
Patty Duke—©Jim Ruymen, Corbis
Indira Gandhi—©Bettman, Corbis
Meryl Streep—©Ken Regan/Paramount Pictures/Bureau L.A. Collections
Natalie Wood—©Douglas Kirkland, Corbis
Photo of Carla Borelli—Courtesy of Carla Borelli
Photo of Laura Huxley—Courtesy of Laura Huxley
Pearls Courtesy of Charmelle Jewelry

Printed in Hong Kong by Graphics Management, Asia, Ltd.

Who ran to help me when I fell,
And would some pretty story tell,
Or kiss the place to make it well?
My Mother.

Ann Taylor 1782-1824 *(My Mother)*

Introduction

Mary True was a very accomplished and well known Baltimore musician. In 1983 *Baltimore Magazine* named her "Baltimore's Best Cocktail Pianist" and in 1989 she received a Congressional Achievement Award praising her for her "exemplary contributions to the field of performing arts." However, the thing of which she was most proud was her family. This is her true legacy. She was my Mother, my confidant, my advisor and my best friend. She was also a best friend to each and every one of her six children. Each of us knew how special we were to her, and it is because of her love and guidance that we learned to love and to look out for each other. Even though she is not physically with us, we share that special bond of caring and love.

My Mother was ageless. She had that marvelous ability to relate to all of her friends and family, no matter what their age. All those who knew my Mother knew her to be a warm and understanding friend. She was never judgmental and always comforting. She was also remarkably intuitive. Somehow she always knew what to say to chase away the blues. My Mother was many things to many people. To some she was the fabulous pianist, Mary True, whose devoted fans would look forward to hearing her play. To others she was a trusted friend and a safe harbor. But, we children always knew that we were the most important people to her. She would always stop what she was doing to share her wisdom and counsel.

My Mother died in 1999 at the age of 83. Although she is no longer with me, I still hear her wonderful words of wisdom in my mind, and I find myself quoting her almost daily.

I dedicate this book to her, and to all the Mothers whose words of wisdom have offered us comfort and guidance through the days of our lives.

—Marie True Evans

ॐ

Quotations from Mary True

Marie True Evans (daughter)

"Be a leader, not a follower."

❧

"Remember not to be overly capable,
or you'll be expected to do it all."

❧

"Find a penny, pick it up,
and all the day you'll have good luck."
*So many times in recent years I have found a
penny on the ground and I've thought,
my Mother must be thinking of me.*

❧

"You can't change yesterday, but you
can change tomorrow by making
right choices today."

❧

Mary True and daughter Marie.

*Whenever someone might be interfering with
another's marriage, or planning on running off
with someone's spouse, my Mother would always say,
"You can never build your happiness
on the unhappiness of others."*

On the unlikely couples:
"There's a lid for every pot."

On hanging around with the wrong crowd:
"Lie down with dogs, come up with fleas."

"Sometimes you gain more by letting go."

"Never marry a man without a sense of humor.
It will carry you through the hard times."

On moving on:
"Living a happy life is the best revenge."

ૐ

"No, is also an answer."

ૐ

"The most important word in a marriage is respect."

ૐ

In troubled times:
"It's always darkest before the dawn."

ૐ

On offering hope:
"When one door closes, another one opens."

ૐ

*My Mother had six children. If all were doing fine
but one, when asked what was wrong, she'd reply,*
"A Mother is only as happy as her unhappiest child."

ૐ

"Be careful what you wish for,
because you just might get it."

On disappointment:
"Never damn your luck."

"If you have to push too hard to make something
happen, it's probably not the right thing."

*Mary True and daughters Marie, Diana
and Adrienne.*

*If one of us kids felt that we were the topic of
conversation, my Mother would say,*
"When they are talking about you,
they're giving some other poor soul a rest."

୬

"Every knock is a boost."

୬

"Better to live in the smallest house
in the best neighborhood,
than to live in the biggest house
in a less desirable one."

୬

" Better to be an old man's darling,
than a young man's fool."

୬

"Don't try to be like everyone else.
Dare to be different."

❧

*Whenever someone became upset about something
that someone had said or something they didn't say,
my Mother would comment,*
"Don't worry so much about what other people
are thinking about you. If the truth be known,
most of the time they are thinking of themselves."

From Diana True Corrigan (daughter)

❧

*Whenever we children would dwell on a subject and
get our needle stuck on*
"woe is me," my Mother would say,
"Put your mind to higher thinking."

From Adrienne Rose True (daughter)

Quotations from
Marie True Evans (Author)

Adrienne Tiffe (daughter)

"You can't do wrong by doing right."

❧

"If it is going to make a difference five years from now,
worry about it. Otherwise, set it aside."

❧

"Don't be a tell all. Remember, what they don't
know can't hurt you."

❧

"If you want to be told what you want to hear,
ask your friends. But, if you want to be told the truth,
ask your Mother."

❧

On staying out late:
"Nothing wholesome ever happens after midnight."

❦

"Time wounds all heels."

❦

"Your life works better when you reserve some time
each day for yourself."

❦

"When you see who a woman lies down with,
you will see her own estimation of herself."

❦

"You don't need to tell the world about your
shortcomings. They will find out for themselves."

❦

"The older I get, the greater the value I place
on my female friendships."

❧

On being a lady:
"Perhaps times have changed, but men have not."

❧

Mary True and Marie True Evans.

"If you feel like your life is out of control and you're
depressed, clean your house.
It's a great remedy."

❧

"Guilt and worry are the two most wasted human
emotions. <u>Guilt</u> is concern over something that
has <u>already</u> happened, and <u>worry</u> is anxiety over
something that may <u>never</u> happen."

❧

"Don't honk your horn at older people.
They could be someone like your Mother or
grandmother—don't honk your horn at <u>anyone</u>."

❧

"In a relationship, remember to reserve something
of yourself for yourself. An air of mystery
is always intriguing."

❧

"Life is what <u>happens</u> to you while you are busy
making other plans."

৵

"Experience is what you <u>get</u> when
you didn't get what you wanted."

৵

"Always put people before profit,
and as a result,
you will build a successful business."

৵

"Remember to be kind to all people—you never know
what is going on in their lives."

৵

"How you end up is usually the realization of how you have envisioned yourself."

About my daughter of two years who stepped
on my bare feet with her high-top shoes:
"She's only stepping on your toes, dear.
Wait 'til she steps on your heart."

— **Nell McInerney**

From Adrienne Tiffe (granddaughter)

Marie True Evans and daughter Adrienne at the celebration of
Maryland's 50th year participation in the Miss America Pagent.

Mother's Pearls

My Mother, Pamela Buffett, always told me,
"You can call me anytime, day or night."
I always knew I was the most important person
in the world to her, and that she truly would be there
for me, and listen when I needed to express
my deepest thoughts and concerns.

From Sarah Buffett (daughter)

When I would be having a particularly difficult time, my
paternal grandmother, Katherine Buffett, would say,
"You can't swim the Atlantic Ocean."
But, with all her love and encouragement,
somehow, I felt I could accomplish anything.

From Sarah Buffett (granddaughter)

During her teenage years, my Mother's father was away as captain of a transport ship in WWII. Her Mother often made the comment that she wished her father were there to help make some of the tough decisions. My dear Mother, Ann Doar Jones, raised my brother and me through the wonderful example of volunteering in the community. One of her memorable quotes that has served me in good stead all these years is:

"If I can't change it, don't tell me what you are going to do before you do it.
Tell me after you have done it."

From Beverley Upshur (daughter)

"Never cry over anything that can't cry over you."

— **Flora Snider**
From Karen Snider (daughter)

"A closed mouth gathers no feet."

— **Katharine Dockman Brooks**

*This was one of my stepmother's favorite mottoes
and it hung on a plaque in our kitchen for many years.
Sometimes we would laugh about it, and sometimes we
wished we had heeded it, so that feelings might not have
been hurt. Or just being silent would have drastically
changed the outcome of a situation much for the better.*
"Be silent and listen."

— **Helen L. Brooks**

8

"If you think you can do something, don't stop, for in
later years you will regret not doing it."

— **Minnie Sekulovich,
Mother of actor Karl Malden**
From Carla Malden (granddaughter)

8

On the many years of friendship:
Without close personal relationships with women,
I would probably not be alive today, and would
certainly not be a vibrant 68-year-old woman. I am
thinking of one relationship, in particular, that has
remained constant over an adult lifespan of 44 years.

We were in our mid-twenties when we met,
both young mothers and both going through some
hard times. Our common interests and struggles
brought us together.

Today, as a clinical psychologist, I have learned
about the power of bonding and attachment in
relationships. We clearly bonded, and that bond
kept us together through all these years. The bond
was like a magic weaving that never broke, because
we knew it kept the tapestry of our lives woven
together and made us complete.

The friendship offered a constant thread of hope and
security through happy times, through very difficult
times, and through all our life changes. We were
always there for each other.

For many years, a long distance friendship was as close as the telephone, or to a treasured visit to spend an extended weekend together. A Christmas gift arrived every year, and birthdays were always remembered. We were an extended family.

My children responded to the bond as they became older, and wrote to my friend. My daughter's letters to her were saved. Several years ago, my older daughter died. A few years later, a lovely scrapbook laced with flowers and her letters arrived as a present to her daughter (my granddaughter). The bonding was passed on to the next generation in a very thoughtful way. Always the message, " I am here for you, always, and I love you." This is the kind of love we need, not only for our personal well-being, but to give to our next generation.

Personal friendships with women are important. They give continuity and meaning to our lives. The love they generate provides the bonding we need to traverse the journey of our lives.

Dr. Barbara Cabott

Regarding the many years of marriage, my Mother called it "A study in mutual tolerance."

— **Cleta Corrigan**
From Mary D'Ambrogi (daughter)

ॐ

"Those who want beautiful hair must be willing to endure having their hair pulled." *My Mother, Lina Pol Perez-Mera, is Spanish, originally from the Dominican Republic. She often used this saying when she was brushing my hair. What I learned from her and this saying was anything worth having in life is usually the result of hard work, and we have to sometimes withstand many obstacles to get what we want and need.*

From Aida Perez-Mera Gamerman (daughter)

ॐ

"Shared joy is doubled, shared sorrow is halved."

— **Petra Obradovich, Serbia**
From Mildred Radovich (daughter)

"You are worthy of all the joy you desire."

— **Joani T. Becker**
From Trish Becker (daughter)

❦"

"No matter how brokenhearted or lonely you may feel, never forget that you are always loved by me."

— **Joani T. Becker**
From Trish Becker (daughter)

❦"

"Yes. Life is like that. You can spend all the time in the world helping others with their work, but you'll still get kicked in the rear for not doing your own."

—**Alice C. Bartlett**
From Trish Becker (granddaughter)

❦

"You cannot change the past, but you can ruin the present by worrying over the future."

—Anonymous

❧

"If you're looking for a good husband—it doesn't matter what he does for a living. What does he do when he's not working?"

—Sophie Alexich
From Mitzi Alexich (daughter)

❧

"Worry is wasting today's time to clutter up tomorrow's opportunities with yesterday's troubles."

— Anonymous

❧

"It's not what you are on the outside, but what you are inside that counts."

—Annette Fass Trustman
From Susan Trustman Leider (daughter)

❧

My favorite saying of my Mother, Annette Fass Trustman, was this wonderful jingle she taught me when I was very young, and later recited so sweetly to my boys. I plan to pass it on to my grandchildren.
"Somebody said it couldn't be done
But with a chuckle replied,
That maybe it couldn't, but he would be one
Who wouldn't say "no" till he tried.
So he buckled right in
With a trace of a grin on his face.
If he worried, he hid it
And he started to sing, as he tackled the thing
That couldn't be done—and he did it!"

From Susan Trustman Leider (daughter)

❧

*Whenever anyone in the family would buy something
and then not be pleased with their purchase, my
Mother-in-law, Anna Center, would say:*
"Soap or no soap—you bought it—you have to eat it."

From Ruth Center (daughter-in-law)

&

"So many people don't like rainy days and they
complain about the weather. I love the rain and it
makes me feel good knowing that the trees, flowers
and crops are being watered."

— Phyllis Miller Jones
From Lavonne Fiore (daughter)

&

I was a serious kid (shy and not giggly) and definitely had little interest in stupid or lazy people. In order to get me to focus more on my studies my Mother would say:
"If you want to attract an intelligent man, you need to study more."

From Leslie Ramsay (daughter)

ॐ

My Mother, Francisca Gamboa, who just celebrated her 90th birthday in the Philippines, was a woman of few words, but I remember her saying: "Be careful who you give your love to, since love always begets love."

She also said:
"Remember, when things don't seem to go right on some days—not all days are Sundays."

And, "If one does not look back to where she came from, she will never get to where she is going."

From Delia Sabundayo (daughter)

ॐ

"Don't let numbers (of people) intimidate you.
You can entertain for fifty as easily as ten—you just
cook more food."

—Phyllis Miller Jones
From Lavonne Fiore, (daughter)

৵

*As I was an only child, my Mother, Flora Fera, and I
were very close. Although she is no longer with us, there
were many bits of wisdom shared between us. I'll always
remember:* "Take great pride in everything you do, no
matter how small the task."

From Leslie Mulcahy (daughter)

৵

*My Mother, Marjorie Oswin Corwin, was born in Bath,
England and moved to America after WWII. She was a
great helper of others. Her words of wisdom were:*
"Take time to do charity, as it is your key to heaven."

From June Hadaway (daughter)

"Be ashamed to die until you've done
something for someone else."

—Rebecca N. Owens
From June Hadaway (great-niece)

❧

"A challenge brings you nutrition for the week."

—Rebecca N. Owens
From June Hadaway (great-niece)

❧

"Eventually you will reach a point when you stop lying
about your age, and start bragging about it."

—Anonymous

❧

The Magic of Colors

"Cheerful colors always create happiness in your mind. Start your day with a colorful breakfast—orange juice, bright fruits, green apples, etc.   Fill your home with colors—cushions, curtains, and bedspreads—colors that make you happy. Look at children—do they choose a colorful toy or a plain gray one? Try to become a child in your mind. Red restores vitality, blue makes you calm, green makes you successful. This works differently for each individual, but look at the rainbow which is an amazing natural creation with all its resplendent colors "

—Lisbeth Silvandersson, Sweden

"Our greatest natural resource is our children."

—Isabel Plaza De Castillo, Colombia, S. A.
From Norma Pelleu (daughter)

"The most powerful channel of
communication
is daily prayer."

—Isabel Plaza De Castillo, Colombia, S. A.
From Norma Pelleu (daughter)

"The most beautiful attire is a smile."

**—Isabel Plaza De Castillo, Colombia,
South America**
From Norma Pelleu (daughter)

"Don't ever write anything and send it if you don't want everyone else to read it."

—Isabel Plaza De Castillo, Colombia, South America
From Norma Pelleu (daughter)

On housework:
"This house will be here long after we're gone—let's just go to the drugstore and have an ice cream soda."

—Dorothy Louise Olson Allison
From Mary Ann Elliot (daughter)

"Ninety-five percent of the things we worry most about never happen—don't fret."

—Dorothy Louise Olson Allison
From Mary Ann Elliot (daughter)

Whenever asked by one of my children which one I loved the most, my reply was, "Well, darlin'—the one I'm with, and right now—that's you."

—Edith Allene Broyhill Stevens
From Mary Ann Elliot

ॐ

My Mother, Poh-Koon Chang, often draws from her deep roots in the Chinese culture to offer words of encouragement and comfort. When I would be going through a disappointing situation, she would say, "Life is like a journey—sometimes very rough, and sometimes very smooth."

From Lydia Cloninger (daughter)

ॐ

"Don't worry about memorizing all the rules. Good manners are simply a matter of being considerate to others."

—Irene Cobots
From Dr. Barbara Cabott (daughter)

"The best thing about grandchildren is that you just have to love them—not worry how they will turn out."

—Eve Bastin
From Ann Shetler (daughter)

❧

"Run rather than walk, help rather than watch others work, act rather than take orders, and do it now rather than tomorrow."

—Joan Simmonds, Middlesex, United Kingdom
From Lauretta Sherman (daughter)

❧

When asked if she would give me away at my wedding, my Mother, Dianne Pierce, replied, "You were never mine to give away. You are God's child. I was just taking care of you."

From Laura Cayouette (daughter)

"Being a step-parent is a decision to go 'all in.'
Kids have amazing detectors for hogwash. You have
to love them with your whole heart if you're going to
love them at all. You can't be a little bit pregnant,
even with someone else's child."

—Laura Cayouette

❧

*In handing down family heirlooms and possessions, it's
better to give them now, rather than leave them in your
will, so you can experience your children enjoying them:*
"I want to give it to you with a warm hand."

—Ida Keller
From Miriam Cohen (niece)

❧

*My Mother would read the newspaper from cover to
cover every morning and then look up and say:*
"Guard your anonymity—stay out of the headlines."
*In being true to her philosophy,
I won't mention her name.*

From Gretchen McCausland (daughter)

"Tell me who your friends are and I'll tell you who you are."

—Olga Kollias, Greece
From Mary Kollias Radovich (daughter)

છે

"Anyone can come to a funeral, bring food when you are sick, etc., and call themselves a friend. A true friend, however, is not just there for you when the chips are down. A true friend rejoices when you rejoice and is elated when good things happen to you. A true friend is happiest when you are happiest."

— Lillian Harder
From Elizabeth Botzis (daughter)

છે

"If you want to have a good time at a party, make sure someone else has a good time."

—Hazel Ives Hutchinson
From Ann Hutchinson Lee (daughter)

A Mother's Advice on Succeeding in Life

"People are often unreasonable, illogical and self-centered —forgive them anyway."
"If you are kind, people may accuse you of selfish ulterior motives —be kind anyway."
"If you are successful, you will win some false friends and some true enemies—succeed anyway."
"If you are honest and frank, people may cheat you —be honest and frank anyway."
"What you spend years building, someone could destroy overnight —build anyway."
"If you find serenity and happiness, there may be jealousy—be happy anyway."
"The good you do today, people will often forget tomorrow—do good anyway."
"Give the world the best you have and it may never be enough—give the world the best you have anyway."
"You see, in the final analysis, it is between you and God—it was never between you and them anyway."

—Author Unknown

In times of concern, my Mother always said:
"Never make a decision at night—the situation
will look different in the morning."

—**Kathy Eaby**

❧

"Character, like sweet herbs should give off its finest
fragrance when pressed."

—**Anonymous**

❧

"It takes 100 years to get to 18, and
18 years to get to 100."

—**Marie Rita Venuto Formiglia, Italy**
From Philomena Formiglia Gorenflo (daughter)

❧

Whenever my Mother, Lora S. Carr, would try to console me in any difficult situation, she would say: "This time next year, you will have a whole different set of worries."

From Leann S. Damico (daughter)

ᏋᎣ

"I'm a Mother, and Mothers know everything." *This explains how my Mother, Lora S. Carr, always knew who broke the figurine, misbehaved in school, or ate all the cookies.*

From Leann S. Damico (daughter)

ᏋᎣ

"The most precious things in life cannot be built by hand or bought by man."

—Anonymous

ᏋᎣ

I was feeling stressed one day with two children in diapers under the age of two. My Mother, Dorothy Gamborg, comforted me by saying, "When your children are small you can solve their problems, but when they grow up you won't be able to solve all of their problems."

From Jeanne Huggins (daughter)

"Life is no bowl of cherries—throw the rottens out, savor the sweet."

—Julia Tohms Olson
From Susan Bolman (daughter)

"Books will always be your best friends. Remember that when you are especially sad."

—Julia Tohms Olson
From Susan Bolman (daughter)

I always told my daughter when she got caught
for some small infraction:
"This is God's way of keeping good people good."

—Lydia Iddings

"You must speak the words that fit into someone
else's ears if you want them to hear you."

—Cornelia Vermeij Moen, Holland
From Dr. Ruth McConnell (daughter)

"You can have whatever you want in this life, but
when you realize the cost to you is when you will
determine how badly you want it."

—Theresa Lubich, Hungary
From Nikki Lubich (daughter)

My mom, Sherry Pyles, always says to me in times of stress, "this too shall pass." Hearing that always makes me feel a little better about the situation. And reflecting back on the situation she's always right and it does pass. As I am older I hear myself saying that in my mind, but in my Mother's voice and that is comforting to me.

From Lyndsay Pyles (daughter)

ﻇ

"The secret of serenity—plan nothing and hang loose."

—Mary Jane (Mike) Flynn

ﻇ

"If St. Peter is going to ask if I did it, then it's important, otherwise let it go."

—Mary Jane (Mike) Flynn

ﻇ

My great-great grandmother,
Margaret Johnston Walker, who was born and lived in
Scotland, wrote this advice to her children:

How To Make a Home Happy:
"Learn to govern yourselves and be gentle and patient.
Guard your tempers, especially in seasons of
ill-health, irritation and trouble, and soften them
by a sense of your own shortcomings and errors."

From Janice Gale (great-great granddaughter)

❧

"Don't wish your life away—enjoy the here and now."

—Mary Edelen McCabe

❧

"Just do your best, and the rest will take
care of itself."

—Grace Abere
From Christine Arnerich (daughter)

Phyllis Diller

Humor

"Always be nice to your children because they are the ones who will choose your rest home."

"Housework can't kill you, but why take a chance?"

"I want my children to have all the things I couldn't afford. Then I want to move in with them."

"Don't go to bed mad—stay up and fight."

—Phyllis Diller

❧

"If at first you don't succeed—try another credit card."

—Mallerie Ettleson
From Laura Ettleson (daughter)

❧

"The older we get, the fewer things seem worth waiting in line for."
—Anonymous

"My Mother, Rose Lampieri, told me,
"Never start your day or leave the house without
putting on your lipstick." To this day, at 87, my
Mother still puts on her lipstick even if she doesn't leave
the apartment at her senior living community.

The perfect example of how right she is reminds me
of when I had very serious back surgery more than
20 years ago. My Mother and father were at my
side every day. After nearly a week of total sedation,
my doctor stopped all medications to monitor my
condition. When my father walked in the room he
took one look at me and completely fell apart. I asked
my Mother to take him out of my room for a minute
and had my nurse help me with my lipstick. When
my parents came back into my room, my father cried
again, only this time he just kept saying over and
over again:
"It's a miracle, it's a miracle—she looks so much
better already."

From Jean Quattlebaum (daughter)

❧

On hurting another person, my Mother,
Cleta Corrigan, said:
"Once you have pulled a person's nose,
you can say you are sorry for pulling their nose,
but their nose is still pulled."

From Mary D'Ambrogi (daughter)

❧

My Mother, Penny DeMar's favorite line and
one that I tell my children as well is,
"To each his own said the old lady
as she kissed the cow."
In other words, everyone is different and what
they like may be different than what you like.

From Rae Ann DeMar (daughter)

❧

"Take advantage of what you are now,
because when you get older your nose gets longer,
your hands get bigger and your feet get wider."

—Kathryn Bilinsky
From Pat Phillips (daughter)

"Stop fussing about not being beautiful—at least you
are not as homely as a mud fence."

—Julia Tohms Olson
From Susan Bolman (daughter)

୬♠

On retaining your beauty:
"Never stand when you can sit—never sit
when you can lie down."

—Anonymous

୬♠

"When you marry—don't ever scrub the first floor or
you will never have scrubbed the last one."

—Marion Hughes
From Bernardine Whitmore (daughter)

୬♠

"If you marry for money alone,
you will earn every penny."

—Anonymous

Grandma's Wisdom

"Whether a man winds up with a nest egg, or a goose egg, depends a lot on the kind of chick he marries."

"Too many couples marry for better or for worse, but not for good."

"When a man marries a woman, they become one; but the trouble starts when they try to decide which one."

"If a man has enough horse sense to treat his wife like a thoroughbred, she will never turn into an old nag."

"The bonds of matrimony are a good investment, but only when the interest is kept up."

"On anniversaries, the wise husband always forgets the past—but never the <u>present</u>."

—Author Unknown

Mother's Teachings

My Mother taught me about HYPOCRISY:
"If I told you once, I've told you a million times,
don't exaggerate!"

My Mother taught me LOGIC:
"Because I said so, that's why."

My Mother taught me ESP:
"Put your sweater on; don't you think
I know when you are cold?"

My Mother taught me WISDOM:
"When you get to be my age, you'll understand."

My Mother taught me about ENVY:
"There are millions of less fortunate children in this
world who don't have wonderful parents like you do."

—Author Unknown

"Peace and war begin at home.

If we truly want peace in the world,
let us begin by loving one another
in our own families. If we want to spread joy,
we need every family to have joy."

—**Mother Teresa**

Quotations from Literary Figures

Laura Huxley

"When do I do the greatest good to myself?"

When do I do the greatest good to others?"

When do I do both, giving and receiving
at the same time?"

—Laura Huxley

ॐ

"Nobody who has not been in the interior of a
family can say what the difficulties of any
individual of that family may be."

—Jane Austin (Emma)

ॐ

"Well, this is the end of a perfect day,
Near the end of a journey, too.
For memory has painted this perfect day
With colors that never fade,
And we find at the end of a perfect day
The soul of a friend we've made."

—Carrie Jacobs Bond—Composer (1862-1946)

"The surest way to get a thing in this life is to be prepared for doing without it, to the exclusion even of hope."

—Jane Welsh Carlyle (1801-1866)

❧

"On the whole a good relationship is one that respects and nourishes the selfhood of the other at the same time it provides the sense of security and at-oneness."

"The point at which you reach maturity is when you forgive your parents."

—Helen Harris Perlman

❧

"One is not born a woman—one becomes one."

—Simone de Beauvoir

"The hardest thing about being a Mother is accepting right down to the bottom of your solar plexus that being a grown-up is not just a phase they're going through and really letting them go."

"I really think now that I'm a grandmother, that children know by three the entire deal and spend the rest of their lives trying to get back to what they were born knowing. The best thing we can do is just not doubt them and allow them to be fully themselves with all the attached messy and often unpleasant feelings and insights. Not indulge them, but not close down their dignity. This is not a job for sissies—this is a life's work for which if you do it right, there will be a good kid at the end of the day."

—Gloria Nagy

❧

"I'll not listen to reason—reason always means what someone else has got to say."

—Elizabeth Cleghorn Gaskell (1810-1865)

❧

"Mothers are the most instinctive philosophers."

—Harriet Beecher Stowe

ॐ

"There are two ways of spreading light: to be the candle or the mirror that reflects it."

—Edith Wharton

ॐ

"The home we first knew of this beautiful earth,
The friends of our childhood, the place of our birth,
In the heart's inner chamber sung always will be,
As the shell ever sings of its home in the sea."
(Home)

—Frances Dana Gage (1808-1884)

ॐ

Quotations from Entertainers

Pearl Bailey

"You never find yourself until you face the truth."

"We look into mirrors but we only see the effects of our times—not our effects on others."

"Everybody wants to do something to help, but nobody wants to be the first."

"Sometimes I would almost rather have people take away years of my life than take away a moment."

"My kitchen is a mystical place, a kind of temple for me. It is a place where the surfaces seem to have significance, where the sounds and the odors carry meaning that transfers to the past and bridges the future."

—Pearl Bailey

ॐ

Patty Duke

"It's toughest to forgive ourselves. So it's probably best to start with other people. It's almost like peeling an onion. Layer by layer, forgiving others you really do get to the point where you can forgive yourself."

"One of the things I've discovered about raising kids is that they really don't give a damn if you walked five miles to school."

—Patty Duke

વ

On remaining humble:
"You can't get spoiled if you do your own ironing."

On overcoming self-doubt:
Even if you are experiencing self-doubt, you can overcome your fear, if you act self-confident. Sometimes we are our own worst critics. Start telling yourself positive thoughts and boost your own self-confidence.

"Fake it till you make it."

—Meryl Streep

Meryl Streep

My Mother, Irene Borelli,
has five children and she would always say:
"Each finger on my hand represents a child—
and if one finger hurts, the whole hand hurts."
This reinforced the fact that we were all
individuals to her but also a family.

—Carla Borelli

Carla Borelli

"The only time a woman succeeds in changing
a man is when he's a baby."

—Natalie Wood

Natalie Wood

My Mother, Vlasta Zuljan,
who is from Slovenia, always said:
"God gave you two ears and one mouth so you
can do twice as much listening as talking."

Now that I am a Mother, I find that I still rely on my
Mother's words when dealing with my own children
and I strive to do more listening than talking.

—Lolita Davidovich

Quotations from First Ladies and Stateswomen

Barbara Bush

"At the end of your life, you will never regret not having passed one more test, not winning one more verdict, or not closing one more deal. You will regret time not spent with a friend, a child, or a parent."

—Barbara Bush

ॐ

"A woman is like a tea bag—you can't tell how strong she is until you put her in hot water."

—Nancy Reagan

President and Mrs. Reagan with Nancy Kennedy, Special Assistant to President Reagan for Legislative Affairs, with goddaughter Adrienne, author's daughter. Taken at the White House Christmas party, 1986.

"It's always been my feeling that God lends
you your children until they're about eighteen
years old. If you haven't made points with them
by then, it's too late."

— Betty Ford

On her formula for molding the
characters of her daughters:
"The giving of love and affection in the home and the
setting of good examples played a major part in their
growth and maturity. Our love for them was strong
and all-encompassing. I think that they, in turn,
developed that same feeling for us, that they wanted
us to be proud of them. If you have love and security
in the home while children are growing up, I suppose
one can cope with almost anything."

— Pat Nixon
McCall's, March, 1969

"A translation from a primitive culture eloquently
describes the importance of our stewardship role in
land use: 'Treat the earth well. It was not given to
us by our parents. It is on loan from our children.'"

—Lady Bird Johnson
AARP convention speech, 1992

෨

"No one can make you feel inferior
without your consent."

"Remember always that you not only have the right to
be an individual—you have an obligation to be one."

"You gain strength, courage and confidence by
every experience in which you really stop to look
fear in the face. You are able to say to yourself,
'I lived through this horror. I can take the next
thing that comes along.' "

—Eleanor Roosevelt

෨

Indira Gandhi

"My grandfather once told me that there were two kinds of people—those who do the work and those who take the credit. He told me to be in the first group—there was much less competition."

"You cannot shake hands with a clenched fist."

—Indira Gandhi

કે

"At work, you think of the children you've left at home. At home, you think of the work you've left unfinished. Such a struggle is unleashed within yourself, your heart is rent."

—Golda Meir

કે

On the importance of female friendships:
Because of a friendship that has spanned over forty
years, I would like to share my thoughts on the
importance of female friendships in our lives. In
addition to loving my own dear Mother—
she was my best friend.

There are various degrees of friendship among
women in general. There are casual friends and
then there are those deep friendships that one can
count on the fingers of one hand. If you are lucky,
you will have one or two. These are the friendships
that endure occasional misunderstandings; that
survive even the most outrageous happenings; that
are as fresh as yesterday when you meet again for
the first time in years. These are the relationships in
which we share the tears of sorrow as well as the tears
of joy. Such is the nature of my friendship with my
best friend, and I am thankful every day for it.

As well, there are the friendships so apparent in
this book, from Mothers of all walks of life. As the
old adage goes, a son is a son till he takes a wife, a
daughter is a daughter for the rest of your life.
Integral to that relationship whose foundation

is love—is the more complicated component of friendship. The lessons learned from the many words of wisdom on these pages cement us to our Mothers in love and friendship in the now and hereafter.

—The Honorable Nancy Mohr Kennedy,
Special Assistant to President Ronald Reagan
for Legislative Affairs

❧

Through the many years of child rearing,
I have always told my children:
"Should you be in any kind of trouble, should anything go awry, make sure that you call me first. Just remember that I am the one who will be in your corner, the one who will have your best interest at heart, and the one who will go to bat for you. There is nothing so bad, that you can't share it with me. Remember that even society's worst offenders also had a Mother."

—Carol Mc Cain,
Director, White House Visitors Office (1981-87)
during the Reagan Years

PSALM CXLIX

PSALM CL.

THE PROVERBS.

CHAP. I.

Proverbs

Proverbs

Proverbs are the daughters of experience.
— *African*

Each day provides its own gifts.
— *American*

Every day of your life is a page of your history.
— *Arabic*

One generation plants the trees; another
gets the shade.
— *Chinese*

Where there is room in the heart there is room
in the house.
— *Danish*

A good name is better than riches.
— *English*

Marriages are made in heaven and
consummated on earth.
— *French*

The old forget, the young don't know.
— *German*

The apple doesn't fall far from the tree.
— *Greek*

Never let on but it's up you're goin.'
— *Irish*

Listen at the keyhole and you'll hear about yourself.
— *Italian*

To love mankind is easy—to love man is hard.
— *Jewish*

Life is like the moon—now full, now dark.
— *Polish*

Give your children too much freedom and
you lose your own.
— *Russian*

An ounce of Mother is worth a pound of clergy.
— *Spanish*

A Mother's Letter

(to a daughter embarking on her career)

My Dearest Daughter,
I was just thinking of my Mother and how I looked to her for her guidance and wise counsel. She was always there for me, and I hope that you know that I am there for you, always. There were so many times in my life that I went to her for comfort and advice. Life isn't always easy, there are many pitfalls and disappointments along with the victories, and we all need to have a Mom to lean on at some time or another.

Now that you are a young adult, I know that this is a new phase of your life filled with new responsibilities. Yet, there is a price to pay for everything that is worthwhile. It all takes care and attention to detail and careful maintenance. Since this is all new to you, I am sure you are feeling a little overwhelmed. But, there is a phrase that goes "How do you eat an elephant? And the answer is - one bite at a time". Since Rome wasn't built in a day, neither is the substance of your life. It's accomplished one building block at a time.

I understand that your current occupation is not your ultimate goal, but it was a very worthwhile endeavor and it is an accomplishment. It has been a new experience and one that has had value. It has been an interesting education and I believe that you have learned much through the training experience.

I certainly value your advice in that field. Also, remember that life is ever changing. You never know where it will take you, and we should all have options to support ourselves in any event. So, the time to learn the trade has been well spent. However, I know that you have aspirations to be working in your chosen field. And that, also, is a good thing, because without goals, we accomplish nothing.

The difference, however, between dreaming and making those dreams a reality is strictly focus and work. My Mother always used to say, "Success in any field is 10% inspiration, 90% perspiration." And how true that statement is for us all. Right now, you have the income from your current business, and the opportunity to grow that business. You are in an excellent position to move forward with your plans. You will need to allow a little time for yourself to enjoy life, and you will need to factor in time to pursue your life's ambition. In order to accomplish all that you wish to achieve, you must make a plan… and that is what I believe is the missing link in your ladder of success. If you don't know where you are going, how will you know when you get there? I do know that nothing is ever accomplished through procrastination. You must set your goals—both short term and long term. Sit down and write your plan for success—daily, weekly, monthly, and yearly. And then follow your plan and be prepared to make adjustments along the way, as needed. What are you going to do each day to bring you closer to success in your chosen field? Be diligent and be organized. Too many things fall through the cracks if you do not have a plan. You also will need to budget your time. Since time is precious, plan what you will do with your 24 daily hours and divide the time appropriately. Plan ahead, and don't procrastinate on anything.

For starters, it means getting and becoming better organized. It means keeping an up-to-date calendar so that you do things in a timely manner, so that you have a daily reminder, instead of being a day late and missing an opportunity. It means making a list of all of your possible contacts in your chosen field and then systematically going about making contact with them to inquire about opportunities. It means becoming better and better about your organizational skills in every way on every day. And remember my motto:

"Do the thing you least want to do the first thing every day and you will feel that the day has been well spent. Procrastinate that which you least want to do and no matter what else you accomplish that day, you will feel that you have accomplished nothing." Eat that elephant one bite at a time, and before you know it, you will be moving in the right direction. By changing the way that you operate, you will change the outcome and achieve your goals. You will be forward moving one step at a time. And take fear out of the equation. Fear nothing but fear itself. You get nothing if you try for nothing. You must be willing to hear "no," in order to get the final "yes!" Be determined and you will succeed in achieving your goals.

Sometimes just making the plan for your future can be overwhelming. But, you do have the experienced travelers along life's road to turn to, your parents. That doesn't mean giving up control of your life—in fact, just the opposite. It means that you recognize the value in asking an experienced traveler the best way to proceed. There is only so much time in life—so don't waste a moment of it on regrets or what-ifs. You need to be proactive about your life. Simply sitting around and wishing, doesn't make it so. It's making a life's plan and implementing that plan on a daily basis. That is very freeing, and far less nerve racking than being helter-skelter. But, with your plan in place, <u>anything</u> is possible.

As my Mother said to me, and I am passing on to you to pass on to your children, "You are the Captain of your ship and the guardian of your fate".

I love you,

Mom

(Anonymous)